My Marathon Journey

Name

My Marathon

Date of Race

MY GOALS

Main Goal

Should do Goal

Must do Goal

Total Dream Goal

TRAINING PYRAMID

Taper
(2 weeks)

Coordination (4 weeks)

Anerobic (4 weeks)

Hills (4 weeks)

Aerobic Base (10 weeks)

The aerobic base is key to marathon success. A less experienced runner will need to extend the base period and reduce the other phases. For a beginner or first time marathon runner I would recommend just following the base training phase.

Over the next few pages I will provide examples of training in each phase that you can adapt to your own ability. If you would like a totally personalised plan contact me through my website www.mattdayrunning.com , let me know you have purchased this training diary and I will give you 10% discount on a personalised plan.

AEROBIC BASE

All running in the initial phase is at a comfortable pace, slowly increasing the times of each run and adjusting to how your body is feeling.

Initial stage

Day 1	Day 2	Day 3	Day 4	Day 5	Day 6	Day 7
30 - 45 mins	30 - 60 mins	30 - 45 mins	30 - 60 mins	30 - 45 mins	30 - 45 mins	45 - 90 mins

As you get fitter

Day 1	Day 2	Day 3	Day 4	Day 5	Day 6	Day 7
60 mins plus some strides	90 mins	60 mins	90 mins	60 mins plus some strides	60 mins easy	120 + mins

More experienced runners would add some Steady state running (building up to 60 mins) within the day 2 and day 4 runs and some easy fartlek on day 3.

You may also wish to add some marathon pace running towards the end of the day 7 long run.

HILL PHASE

Day 1	Day 2	Day 3	Day 4	Day 5	Day 6	Day 7
30 - 60 mins with 6 - 10 x 100m with full recovery between each 100m leg speed effort	30 - 60 mins hill exercises / circuit	30 - 60 mins	30 - 60 mins hill exercises / circuit	30 - 60 mins	30 - 60 mins easy	120 + mins

ANAEROBIC PHASE

Day 1	Day 2	Day 3	Day 4	Day 5	Day 6	Day 7
30 - 60 mins	Longer Intervals	30 - 60 mins	Shorter Intervals	30 - 60 mins	30 - 60 mins easy or 5k / 10k time trial at ¾ effort	120 + mins

COORDINATION PHASE

Day 1	Day 2	Day 3	Day 4	Day 5	Day 6	Day 7
30 - 60 mins	3k to 5k time trial	60 - 90 mins	45 - 60 mins with some strides	3k to 5k time trial	30 - 60 mins	120 + mins with some marathon paced sections within the run.

TAPER

Day 1	Day 2	Day 3	Day 4	Day 5	Day 6	Day 7
100m fast 100m float x 10 -12	Easy 60 - 90 mins	3k to 5k time trial	45 - 60 ns with some strides	Easy 45 - 60 mins	3k to 5k at marathon pace	60 - 90 mins easy
30 - 60 mins with 6 x 100m with full recovery between each	2-3k at marathon pace	Easy 45 mins	Easy 30 mins	Easy 30 mins	Easy 15 - 30 mins	RACE DAY

If you have any questions about any aspects of this outline training plan please do contact me through my website and I will always be happy to answer any questions.

www.mattdayrunning.com

WEEK 1

DAY 1

TIME OF DAY	ROUTE	DISTANCE	TIME

PACE	HEART RATE	WEATHER	SHOES

COMMENTS

ADDITIONAL RUN OR CROSS TRAINING			
TIME OF DAY	ROUTE	DISTANCE	TIME
PACE	HEART RATE	WEATHER	SHOES

COMMENTS

DAY 2

TIME OF DAY	ROUTE	DISTANCE	TIME
PACE	HEART RATE	WEATHER	SHOES

COMMENTS

ADDITIONAL RUN OR CROSS TRAINING			
TIME OF DAY	ROUTE	DISTANCE	TIME
PACE	HEART RATE	WEATHER	SHOES

COMMENTS

DAY 3

TIME OF DAY	ROUTE	DISTANCE	TIME

PACE	HEART RATE	WEATHER	SHOES

COMMENTS

ADDITIONAL RUN OR CROSS TRAINING			
TIME OF DAY	ROUTE	DISTANCE	TIME
PACE	HEART RATE	WEATHER	SHOES

COMMENTS

DAY 4

TIME OF DAY	ROUTE	DISTANCE	TIME

PACE	HEART RATE	WEATHER	SHOES

COMMENTS

ADDITIONAL RUN OR CROSS TRAINING			
TIME OF DAY	ROUTE	DISTANCE	TIME
PACE	HEART RATE	WEATHER	SHOES

COMMENTS

DAY 5

TIME OF DAY	ROUTE	DISTANCE	TIME
PACE	HEART RATE	WEATHER	SHOES

COMMENTS

ADDITIONAL RUN OR CROSS TRAINING			
TIME OF DAY	ROUTE	DISTANCE	TIME
PACE	HEART RATE	WEATHER	SHOES

COMMENTS

DAY 6

TIME OF DAY	ROUTE	DISTANCE	TIME
PACE	HEART RATE	WEATHER	SHOES

COMMENTS

ADDITIONAL RUN OR CROSS TRAINING			
TIME OF DAY	ROUTE	DISTANCE	TIME
PACE	HEART RATE	WEATHER	SHOES

COMMENTS

DAY 7	TIME OF DAY	ROUTE	DISTANCE	TIME
	PACE	HEART RATE	WEATHER	SHOES
	COMMENTS			
	ADDITIONAL RUN OR CROSS TRAINING			
	TIME OF DAY	ROUTE	DISTANCE	TIME
	PACE	HEART RATE	WEATHER	SHOES
	COMMENTS			

SUMMARY OF WEEK

RUNNING

TOTAL TIME	TOTAL DISTANCE

CROSS TRAINING

TOTAL TIME	TOTAL DISTANCE

STRENGTH & CONDITIONING

TOTAL TIME

REVIEW OF THE WEEK

HOW I FEEL PHYSICALLY

HOW I FEEL MENTALLY

HIGHLIGHTS OF THE WEEK

WEEK 2

DAY 1

TIME OF DAY	ROUTE	DISTANCE	TIME

PACE	HEART RATE	WEATHER	SHOES

COMMENTS

ADDITIONAL RUN OR CROSS TRAINING			
TIME OF DAY	ROUTE	DISTANCE	TIME
PACE	HEART RATE	WEATHER	SHOES

COMMENTS

DAY 2

TIME OF DAY	ROUTE	DISTANCE	TIME

PACE	HEART RATE	WEATHER	SHOES

COMMENTS

ADDITIONAL RUN OR CROSS TRAINING			
TIME OF DAY	ROUTE	DISTANCE	TIME
PACE	HEART RATE	WEATHER	SHOES

COMMENTS

DAY 3

TIME OF DAY	ROUTE	DISTANCE	TIME

PACE	HEART RATE	WEATHER	SHOES

COMMENTS

ADDITIONAL RUN OR CROSS TRAINING			
TIME OF DAY	ROUTE	DISTANCE	TIME
PACE	HEART RATE	WEATHER	SHOES

COMMENTS

DAY 4

TIME OF DAY	ROUTE	DISTANCE	TIME

PACE	HEART RATE	WEATHER	SHOES

COMMENTS

ADDITIONAL RUN OR CROSS TRAINING			
TIME OF DAY	ROUTE	DISTANCE	TIME
PACE	HEART RATE	WEATHER	SHOES

COMMENTS

DAY 5

TIME OF DAY	ROUTE	DISTANCE	TIME
PACE	HEART RATE	WEATHER	SHOES

COMMENTS

ADDITIONAL RUN OR CROSS TRAINING			
TIME OF DAY	ROUTE	DISTANCE	TIME
PACE	HEART RATE	WEATHER	SHOES

COMMENTS

DAY 6

TIME OF DAY	ROUTE	DISTANCE	TIME
PACE	HEART RATE	WEATHER	SHOES

COMMENTS

ADDITIONAL RUN OR CROSS TRAINING			
TIME OF DAY	ROUTE	DISTANCE	TIME
PACE	HEART RATE	WEATHER	SHOES

COMMENTS

DAY 7	TIME OF DAY	ROUTE	DISTANCE	TIME
	PACE	HEART RATE	WEATHER	SHOES

COMMENTS

ADDITIONAL RUN OR CROSS TRAINING			
TIME OF DAY	ROUTE	DISTANCE	TIME
PACE	HEART RATE	WEATHER	SHOES

COMMENTS

SUMMARY OF WEEK

RUNNING

TOTAL TIME

TOTAL DISTANCE

CROSS TRAINING

TOTAL TIME

TOTAL DISTANCE

STRENGTH & CONDITIONING

TOTAL TIME

REVIEW OF THE WEEK

HOW I FEEL PHYSICALLY

HOW I FEEL MENTALLY

HIGHLIGHTS OF THE WEEK

WEEK 3

DAY 1

TIME OF DAY	ROUTE	DISTANCE	TIME

PACE	HEART RATE	WEATHER	SHOES

COMMENTS

ADDITIONAL RUN OR CROSS TRAINING			
TIME OF DAY	ROUTE	DISTANCE	TIME
PACE	HEART RATE	WEATHER	SHOES

COMMENTS

DAY 2

TIME OF DAY	ROUTE	DISTANCE	TIME

PACE	HEART RATE	WEATHER	SHOES

COMMENTS

ADDITIONAL RUN OR CROSS TRAINING			
TIME OF DAY	ROUTE	DISTANCE	TIME
PACE	HEART RATE	WEATHER	SHOES

COMMENTS

DAY 3

TIME OF DAY	ROUTE	DISTANCE	TIME

PACE	HEART RATE	WEATHER	SHOES

COMMENTS

ADDITIONAL RUN OR CROSS TRAINING			
TIME OF DAY	ROUTE	DISTANCE	TIME
PACE	HEART RATE	WEATHER	SHOES

COMMENTS

DAY 4

TIME OF DAY	ROUTE	DISTANCE	TIME

PACE	HEART RATE	WEATHER	SHOES

COMMENTS

ADDITIONAL RUN OR CROSS TRAINING			
TIME OF DAY	ROUTE	DISTANCE	TIME
PACE	HEART RATE	WEATHER	SHOES

COMMENTS

DAY 5

TIME OF DAY	ROUTE	DISTANCE	TIME

PACE	HEART RATE	WEATHER	SHOES

COMMENTS

ADDITIONAL RUN OR CROSS TRAINING			
TIME OF DAY	ROUTE	DISTANCE	TIME
PACE	HEART RATE	WEATHER	SHOES

COMMENTS

DAY 6

TIME OF DAY	ROUTE	DISTANCE	TIME

PACE	HEART RATE	WEATHER	SHOES

COMMENTS

ADDITIONAL RUN OR CROSS TRAINING			
TIME OF DAY	ROUTE	DISTANCE	TIME
PACE	HEART RATE	WEATHER	SHOES

COMMENTS

DAY 7	TIME OF DAY	ROUTE	DISTANCE	TIME
	PACE	HEART RATE	WEATHER	SHOES
	COMMENTS			
	ADDITIONAL RUN OR CROSS TRAINING			
	TIME OF DAY	ROUTE	DISTANCE	TIME
	PACE	HEART RATE	WEATHER	SHOES
	COMMENTS			

SUMMARY OF WEEK

RUNNING

TOTAL TIME	TOTAL DISTANCE

CROSS TRAINING

TOTAL TIME	TOTAL DISTANCE

STRENGTH & CONDITIONING

TOTAL TIME

REVIEW OF THE WEEK

HOW I FEEL PHYSICALLY

HOW I FEEL MENTALLY

HIGHLIGHTS OF THE WEEK

WEEK 4

DAY 1

TIME OF DAY	ROUTE	DISTANCE	TIME

PACE	HEART RATE	WEATHER	SHOES

COMMENTS

ADDITIONAL RUN OR CROSS TRAINING			
TIME OF DAY	ROUTE	DISTANCE	TIME
PACE	HEART RATE	WEATHER	SHOES

COMMENTS

DAY 2

TIME OF DAY	ROUTE	DISTANCE	TIME
PACE	HEART RATE	WEATHER	SHOES

COMMENTS

ADDITIONAL RUN OR CROSS TRAINING			
TIME OF DAY	ROUTE	DISTANCE	TIME
PACE	HEART RATE	WEATHER	SHOES

COMMENTS

DAY 3

TIME OF DAY	ROUTE	DISTANCE	TIME

PACE	HEART RATE	WEATHER	SHOES

COMMENTS

ADDITIONAL RUN OR CROSS TRAINING			
TIME OF DAY	ROUTE	DISTANCE	TIME
PACE	HEART RATE	WEATHER	SHOES

COMMENTS

DAY 4

TIME OF DAY	ROUTE	DISTANCE	TIME
PACE	HEART RATE	WEATHER	SHOES

COMMENTS

ADDITIONAL RUN OR CROSS TRAINING			
TIME OF DAY	ROUTE	DISTANCE	TIME
PACE	HEART RATE	WEATHER	SHOES

COMMENTS

DAY 5

TIME OF DAY	ROUTE	DISTANCE	TIME

PACE	HEART RATE	WEATHER	SHOES

COMMENTS

ADDITIONAL RUN OR CROSS TRAINING			
TIME OF DAY	ROUTE	DISTANCE	TIME
PACE	HEART RATE	WEATHER	SHOES

COMMENTS

DAY 6

TIME OF DAY	ROUTE	DISTANCE	TIME

PACE	HEART RATE	WEATHER	SHOES

COMMENTS

ADDITIONAL RUN OR CROSS TRAINING			
TIME OF DAY	ROUTE	DISTANCE	TIME
PACE	HEART RATE	WEATHER	SHOES

COMMENTS

DAY 7	TIME OF DAY	ROUTE	DISTANCE	TIME
	PACE	HEART RATE	WEATHER	SHOES
	COMMENTS			

ADDITIONAL RUN OR CROSS TRAINING			
TIME OF DAY	ROUTE	DISTANCE	TIME
PACE	HEART RATE	WEATHER	SHOES
COMMENTS			

SUMMARY OF WEEK

RUNNING

TOTAL TIME	TOTAL DISTANCE

CROSS TRAINING

TOTAL TIME	TOTAL DISTANCE

STRENGTH & CONDITIONING

TOTAL TIME

REVIEW OF THE WEEK

HOW I FEEL PHYSICALLY

HOW I FEEL MENTALLY

HIGHLIGHTS OF THE WEEK

WEEK 5

DAY 1

TIME OF DAY	ROUTE	DISTANCE	TIME

PACE	HEART RATE	WEATHER	SHOES

COMMENTS

ADDITIONAL RUN OR CROSS TRAINING			
TIME OF DAY	ROUTE	DISTANCE	TIME
PACE	HEART RATE	WEATHER	SHOES

COMMENTS

DAY 2

TIME OF DAY	ROUTE	DISTANCE	TIME

PACE	HEART RATE	WEATHER	SHOES

COMMENTS

ADDITIONAL RUN OR CROSS TRAINING			
TIME OF DAY	ROUTE	DISTANCE	TIME
PACE	HEART RATE	WEATHER	SHOES

COMMENTS

DAY 3

TIME OF DAY	ROUTE	DISTANCE	TIME

PACE	HEART RATE	WEATHER	SHOES

COMMENTS

ADDITIONAL RUN OR CROSS TRAINING			
TIME OF DAY	ROUTE	DISTANCE	TIME
PACE	HEART RATE	WEATHER	SHOES

COMMENTS

DAY 4

TIME OF DAY	ROUTE	DISTANCE	TIME

PACE	HEART RATE	WEATHER	SHOES

COMMENTS

ADDITIONAL RUN OR CROSS TRAINING			
TIME OF DAY	ROUTE	DISTANCE	TIME
PACE	HEART RATE	WEATHER	SHOES

COMMENTS

DAY 5

	TIME OF DAY	ROUTE	DISTANCE	TIME
	PACE	HEART RATE	WEATHER	SHOES

COMMENTS

ADDITIONAL RUN OR CROSS TRAINING			
TIME OF DAY	ROUTE	DISTANCE	TIME
PACE	HEART RATE	WEATHER	SHOES

COMMENTS

DAY 6

	TIME OF DAY	ROUTE	DISTANCE	TIME
	PACE	HEART RATE	WEATHER	SHOES

COMMENTS

ADDITIONAL RUN OR CROSS TRAINING			
TIME OF DAY	ROUTE	DISTANCE	TIME
PACE	HEART RATE	WEATHER	SHOES

COMMENTS

DAY 7	TIME OF DAY	ROUTE	DISTANCE	TIME
	PACE	HEART RATE	WEATHER	SHOES
	COMMENTS			

ADDITIONAL RUN OR CROSS TRAINING

TIME OF DAY	ROUTE	DISTANCE	TIME
PACE	HEART RATE	WEATHER	SHOES
COMMENTS			

SUMMARY OF WEEK

RUNNING

TOTAL TIME

TOTAL DISTANCE

CROSS TRAINING

TOTAL TIME

TOTAL DISTANCE

STRENGTH & CONDITIONING

TOTAL TIME

REVIEW OF THE WEEK

HOW I FEEL PHYSICALLY

HOW I FEEL MENTALLY

HIGHLIGHTS OF THE WEEK

WEEK 6

DAY 1

TIME OF DAY	ROUTE	DISTANCE	TIME

PACE	HEART RATE	WEATHER	SHOES

COMMENTS

ADDITIONAL RUN OR CROSS TRAINING			
TIME OF DAY	ROUTE	DISTANCE	TIME
PACE	HEART RATE	WEATHER	SHOES

COMMENTS

DAY 2

TIME OF DAY	ROUTE	DISTANCE	TIME
PACE	HEART RATE	WEATHER	SHOES

COMMENTS

ADDITIONAL RUN OR CROSS TRAINING			
TIME OF DAY	ROUTE	DISTANCE	TIME
PACE	HEART RATE	WEATHER	SHOES

COMMENTS

DAY 3

TIME OF DAY	ROUTE	DISTANCE	TIME

PACE	HEART RATE	WEATHER	SHOES

COMMENTS

ADDITIONAL RUN OR CROSS TRAINING			
TIME OF DAY	ROUTE	DISTANCE	TIME
PACE	HEART RATE	WEATHER	SHOES

COMMENTS

DAY 4

TIME OF DAY	ROUTE	DISTANCE	TIME

PACE	HEART RATE	WEATHER	SHOES

COMMENTS

ADDITIONAL RUN OR CROSS TRAINING			
TIME OF DAY	ROUTE	DISTANCE	TIME
PACE	HEART RATE	WEATHER	SHOES

COMMENTS

DAY 5

TIME OF DAY	ROUTE	DISTANCE	TIME

PACE	HEART RATE	WEATHER	SHOES

COMMENTS

ADDITIONAL RUN OR CROSS TRAINING			
TIME OF DAY	ROUTE	DISTANCE	TIME
PACE	HEART RATE	WEATHER	SHOES

COMMENTS

DAY 6

TIME OF DAY	ROUTE	DISTANCE	TIME

PACE	HEART RATE	WEATHER	SHOES

COMMENTS

ADDITIONAL RUN OR CROSS TRAINING			
TIME OF DAY	ROUTE	DISTANCE	TIME
PACE	HEART RATE	WEATHER	SHOES

COMMENTS

DAY 7	TIME OF DAY	ROUTE	DISTANCE	TIME
	PACE	HEART RATE	WEATHER	SHOES

COMMENTS

ADDITIONAL RUN OR CROSS TRAINING			
TIME OF DAY	ROUTE	DISTANCE	TIME
PACE	HEART RATE	WEATHER	SHOES

COMMENTS

SUMMARY OF WEEK

RUNNING

TOTAL TIME	TOTAL DISTANCE

CROSS TRAINING

TOTAL TIME	TOTAL DISTANCE

STRENGTH & CONDITIONING

TOTAL TIME

REVIEW OF THE WEEK

HOW I FEEL PHYSICALLY

HOW I FEEL MENTALLY

HIGHLIGHTS OF THE WEEK

WEEK 7

DAY 1

TIME OF DAY	ROUTE	DISTANCE	TIME

PACE	HEART RATE	WEATHER	SHOES

COMMENTS

ADDITIONAL RUN OR CROSS TRAINING			
TIME OF DAY	ROUTE	DISTANCE	TIME
PACE	HEART RATE	WEATHER	SHOES

COMMENTS

DAY 2

TIME OF DAY	ROUTE	DISTANCE	TIME

PACE	HEART RATE	WEATHER	SHOES

COMMENTS

ADDITIONAL RUN OR CROSS TRAINING			
TIME OF DAY	ROUTE	DISTANCE	TIME
PACE	HEART RATE	WEATHER	SHOES

COMMENTS

DAY 3

TIME OF DAY	ROUTE	DISTANCE	TIME

PACE	HEART RATE	WEATHER	SHOES

COMMENTS

ADDITIONAL RUN OR CROSS TRAINING			
TIME OF DAY	ROUTE	DISTANCE	TIME
PACE	HEART RATE	WEATHER	SHOES

COMMENTS

DAY 4

TIME OF DAY	ROUTE	DISTANCE	TIME
PACE	HEART RATE	WEATHER	SHOES

COMMENTS

ADDITIONAL RUN OR CROSS TRAINING			
TIME OF DAY	ROUTE	DISTANCE	TIME
PACE	HEART RATE	WEATHER	SHOES

COMMENTS

DAY 5

TIME OF DAY	ROUTE	DISTANCE	TIME

PACE	HEART RATE	WEATHER	SHOES

COMMENTS

ADDITIONAL RUN OR CROSS TRAINING			
TIME OF DAY	ROUTE	DISTANCE	TIME
PACE	HEART RATE	WEATHER	SHOES

COMMENTS

DAY 6

TIME OF DAY	ROUTE	DISTANCE	TIME

PACE	HEART RATE	WEATHER	SHOES

COMMENTS

ADDITIONAL RUN OR CROSS TRAINING			
TIME OF DAY	ROUTE	DISTANCE	TIME
PACE	HEART RATE	WEATHER	SHOES

COMMENTS

DAY 7	TIME OF DAY	ROUTE	DISTANCE	TIME
	PACE	HEART RATE	WEATHER	SHOES
	COMMENTS			

ADDITIONAL RUN OR CROSS TRAINING			
TIME OF DAY	ROUTE	DISTANCE	TIME
PACE	HEART RATE	WEATHER	SHOES
COMMENTS			

SUMMARY OF WEEK

RUNNING

TOTAL TIME	TOTAL DISTANCE

CROSS TRAINING

TOTAL TIME	TOTAL DISTANCE

STRENGTH & CONDITIONING

TOTAL TIME

REVIEW OF THE WEEK

HOW I FEEL PHYSICALLY

HOW I FEEL MENTALLY

HIGHLIGHTS OF THE WEEK

WEEK 8

DAY 1

TIME OF DAY	ROUTE	DISTANCE	TIME

PACE	HEART RATE	WEATHER	SHOES

COMMENTS

ADDITIONAL RUN OR CROSS TRAINING			
TIME OF DAY	ROUTE	DISTANCE	TIME
PACE	HEART RATE	WEATHER	SHOES

COMMENTS

DAY 2

TIME OF DAY	ROUTE	DISTANCE	TIME

PACE	HEART RATE	WEATHER	SHOES

COMMENTS

ADDITIONAL RUN OR CROSS TRAINING			
TIME OF DAY	ROUTE	DISTANCE	TIME
PACE	HEART RATE	WEATHER	SHOES

COMMENTS

DAY 3

TIME OF DAY	ROUTE	DISTANCE	TIME

PACE	HEART RATE	WEATHER	SHOES

COMMENTS

ADDITIONAL RUN OR CROSS TRAINING			
TIME OF DAY	ROUTE	DISTANCE	TIME
PACE	HEART RATE	WEATHER	SHOES

COMMENTS

DAY 4

TIME OF DAY	ROUTE	DISTANCE	TIME
PACE	HEART RATE	WEATHER	SHOES

COMMENTS

ADDITIONAL RUN OR CROSS TRAINING			
TIME OF DAY	ROUTE	DISTANCE	TIME
PACE	HEART RATE	WEATHER	SHOES

COMMENTS

DAY 5

TIME OF DAY	ROUTE	DISTANCE	TIME
PACE	HEART RATE	WEATHER	SHOES

COMMENTS

ADDITIONAL RUN OR CROSS TRAINING			
TIME OF DAY	ROUTE	DISTANCE	TIME
PACE	HEART RATE	WEATHER	SHOES

COMMENTS

DAY 6

TIME OF DAY	ROUTE	DISTANCE	TIME
PACE	HEART RATE	WEATHER	SHOES

COMMENTS

ADDITIONAL RUN OR CROSS TRAINING			
TIME OF DAY	ROUTE	DISTANCE	TIME
PACE	HEART RATE	WEATHER	SHOES

COMMENTS

DAY 7	TIME OF DAY	ROUTE	DISTANCE	TIME
	PACE	HEART RATE	WEATHER	SHOES

COMMENTS

ADDITIONAL RUN OR CROSS TRAINING			
TIME OF DAY	ROUTE	DISTANCE	TIME
PACE	HEART RATE	WEATHER	SHOES

COMMENTS

SUMMARY OF WEEK

RUNNING

TOTAL TIME   TOTAL DISTANCE

CROSS TRAINING

TOTAL TIME   TOTAL DISTANCE

STRENGTH & CONDITIONING

TOTAL TIME

REVIEW OF THE WEEK

HOW I FEEL PHYSICALLY

HOW I FEEL MENTALLY

HIGHLIGHTS OF THE WEEK

WEEK 9

DAY 1

TIME OF DAY	ROUTE	DISTANCE	TIME

PACE	HEART RATE	WEATHER	SHOES

COMMENTS

ADDITIONAL RUN OR CROSS TRAINING			
TIME OF DAY	ROUTE	DISTANCE	TIME
PACE	HEART RATE	WEATHER	SHOES

COMMENTS

DAY 2

TIME OF DAY	ROUTE	DISTANCE	TIME

PACE	HEART RATE	WEATHER	SHOES

COMMENTS

ADDITIONAL RUN OR CROSS TRAINING			
TIME OF DAY	ROUTE	DISTANCE	TIME
PACE	HEART RATE	WEATHER	SHOES

COMMENTS

DAY 3

TIME OF DAY	ROUTE	DISTANCE	TIME

PACE	HEART RATE	WEATHER	SHOES

COMMENTS

ADDITIONAL RUN OR CROSS TRAINING			
TIME OF DAY	ROUTE	DISTANCE	TIME
PACE	HEART RATE	WEATHER	SHOES

COMMENTS

DAY 4

TIME OF DAY	ROUTE	DISTANCE	TIME

PACE	HEART RATE	WEATHER	SHOES

COMMENTS

ADDITIONAL RUN OR CROSS TRAINING			
TIME OF DAY	ROUTE	DISTANCE	TIME
PACE	HEART RATE	WEATHER	SHOES

COMMENTS

DAY 5

TIME OF DAY	ROUTE	DISTANCE	TIME

PACE	HEART RATE	WEATHER	SHOES

COMMENTS

ADDITIONAL RUN OR CROSS TRAINING			
TIME OF DAY	ROUTE	DISTANCE	TIME
PACE	HEART RATE	WEATHER	SHOES

COMMENTS

DAY 6

TIME OF DAY	ROUTE	DISTANCE	TIME

PACE	HEART RATE	WEATHER	SHOES

COMMENTS

ADDITIONAL RUN OR CROSS TRAINING			
TIME OF DAY	ROUTE	DISTANCE	TIME
PACE	HEART RATE	WEATHER	SHOES

COMMENTS

DAY 7	TIME OF DAY	ROUTE	DISTANCE	TIME
	PACE	HEART RATE	WEATHER	SHOES
	COMMENTS			

ADDITIONAL RUN OR CROSS TRAINING			
TIME OF DAY	ROUTE	DISTANCE	TIME
PACE	HEART RATE	WEATHER	SHOES
COMMENTS			

SUMMARY OF WEEK

RUNNING

TOTAL TIME	TOTAL DISTANCE

CROSS TRAINING

TOTAL TIME	TOTAL DISTANCE

STRENGTH & CONDITIONING

TOTAL TIME

REVIEW OF THE WEEK

HOW I FEEL PHYSICALLY

HOW I FEEL MENTALLY

HIGHLIGHTS OF THE WEEK

WEEK 10

DAY 1

TIME OF DAY	ROUTE	DISTANCE	TIME

PACE	HEART RATE	WEATHER	SHOES

COMMENTS

ADDITIONAL RUN OR CROSS TRAINING			
TIME OF DAY	ROUTE	DISTANCE	TIME
PACE	HEART RATE	WEATHER	SHOES

COMMENTS

DAY 2

TIME OF DAY	ROUTE	DISTANCE	TIME

PACE	HEART RATE	WEATHER	SHOES

COMMENTS

ADDITIONAL RUN OR CROSS TRAINING			
TIME OF DAY	ROUTE	DISTANCE	TIME
PACE	HEART RATE	WEATHER	SHOES

COMMENTS

DAY 3

TIME OF DAY	ROUTE	DISTANCE	TIME
PACE	HEART RATE	WEATHER	SHOES

COMMENTS

ADDITIONAL RUN OR CROSS TRAINING			
TIME OF DAY	ROUTE	DISTANCE	TIME
PACE	HEART RATE	WEATHER	SHOES

COMMENTS

DAY 4

TIME OF DAY	ROUTE	DISTANCE	TIME
PACE	HEART RATE	WEATHER	SHOES

COMMENTS

ADDITIONAL RUN OR CROSS TRAINING			
TIME OF DAY	ROUTE	DISTANCE	TIME
PACE	HEART RATE	WEATHER	SHOES

COMMENTS

DAY 5

TIME OF DAY	ROUTE	DISTANCE	TIME

PACE	HEART RATE	WEATHER	SHOES

COMMENTS

ADDITIONAL RUN OR CROSS TRAINING			
TIME OF DAY	ROUTE	DISTANCE	TIME
PACE	HEART RATE	WEATHER	SHOES

COMMENTS

DAY 6

TIME OF DAY	ROUTE	DISTANCE	TIME

PACE	HEART RATE	WEATHER	SHOES

COMMENTS

ADDITIONAL RUN OR CROSS TRAINING			
TIME OF DAY	ROUTE	DISTANCE	TIME
PACE	HEART RATE	WEATHER	SHOES

COMMENTS

DAY 7	TIME OF DAY	ROUTE	DISTANCE	TIME
	PACE	HEART RATE	WEATHER	SHOES

COMMENTS

ADDITIONAL RUN OR CROSS TRAINING			
TIME OF DAY	ROUTE	DISTANCE	TIME
PACE	HEART RATE	WEATHER	SHOES

COMMENTS

SUMMARY OF WEEK

RUNNING

TOTAL TIME	TOTAL DISTANCE

CROSS TRAINING

TOTAL TIME	TOTAL DISTANCE

STRENGTH & CONDITIONING

TOTAL TIME

REVIEW OF THE WEEK

HOW I FEEL PHYSICALLY

HOW I FEEL MENTALLY

HIGHLIGHTS OF THE WEEK

WEEK 11

DAY 1

TIME OF DAY	ROUTE	DISTANCE	TIME

PACE	HEART RATE	WEATHER	SHOES

COMMENTS

ADDITIONAL RUN OR CROSS TRAINING			
TIME OF DAY	ROUTE	DISTANCE	TIME
PACE	HEART RATE	WEATHER	SHOES

COMMENTS

DAY 2

TIME OF DAY	ROUTE	DISTANCE	TIME

PACE	HEART RATE	WEATHER	SHOES

COMMENTS

ADDITIONAL RUN OR CROSS TRAINING			
TIME OF DAY	ROUTE	DISTANCE	TIME
PACE	HEART RATE	WEATHER	SHOES

COMMENTS

DAY 3

TIME OF DAY	ROUTE	DISTANCE	TIME

PACE	HEART RATE	WEATHER	SHOES

COMMENTS

ADDITIONAL RUN OR CROSS TRAINING			
TIME OF DAY	ROUTE	DISTANCE	TIME
PACE	HEART RATE	WEATHER	SHOES

COMMENTS

DAY 4

TIME OF DAY	ROUTE	DISTANCE	TIME
PACE	HEART RATE	WEATHER	SHOES

COMMENTS

ADDITIONAL RUN OR CROSS TRAINING			
TIME OF DAY	ROUTE	DISTANCE	TIME
PACE	HEART RATE	WEATHER	SHOES

COMMENTS

DAY 5

TIME OF DAY	ROUTE	DISTANCE	TIME

PACE	HEART RATE	WEATHER	SHOES

COMMENTS

ADDITIONAL RUN OR CROSS TRAINING			
TIME OF DAY	ROUTE	DISTANCE	TIME
PACE	HEART RATE	WEATHER	SHOES

COMMENTS

DAY 6

TIME OF DAY	ROUTE	DISTANCE	TIME

PACE	HEART RATE	WEATHER	SHOES

COMMENTS

ADDITIONAL RUN OR CROSS TRAINING			
TIME OF DAY	ROUTE	DISTANCE	TIME
PACE	HEART RATE	WEATHER	SHOES

COMMENTS

DAY 7	TIME OF DAY	ROUTE	DISTANCE	TIME
	PACE	HEART RATE	WEATHER	SHOES
	COMMENTS			

ADDITIONAL RUN OR CROSS TRAINING			
TIME OF DAY	ROUTE	DISTANCE	TIME
PACE	HEART RATE	WEATHER	SHOES
COMMENTS			

SUMMARY OF WEEK

RUNNING

TOTAL TIME	TOTAL DISTANCE

CROSS TRAINING

TOTAL TIME	TOTAL DISTANCE

STRENGTH & CONDITIONING

TOTAL TIME

REVIEW OF THE WEEK

HOW I FEEL PHYSICALLY

HOW I FEEL MENTALLY

HIGHLIGHTS OF THE WEEK

WEEK 12

DAY 1

TIME OF DAY	ROUTE	DISTANCE	TIME

PACE	HEART RATE	WEATHER	SHOES

COMMENTS

ADDITIONAL RUN OR CROSS TRAINING			
TIME OF DAY	ROUTE	DISTANCE	TIME
PACE	HEART RATE	WEATHER	SHOES

COMMENTS

DAY 2

TIME OF DAY	ROUTE	DISTANCE	TIME
PACE	HEART RATE	WEATHER	SHOES

COMMENTS

ADDITIONAL RUN OR CROSS TRAINING			
TIME OF DAY	ROUTE	DISTANCE	TIME
PACE	HEART RATE	WEATHER	SHOES

COMMENTS

DAY 3

TIME OF DAY	ROUTE	DISTANCE	TIME

PACE	HEART RATE	WEATHER	SHOES

COMMENTS

ADDITIONAL RUN OR CROSS TRAINING			
TIME OF DAY	ROUTE	DISTANCE	TIME
PACE	HEART RATE	WEATHER	SHOES

COMMENTS

DAY 4

TIME OF DAY	ROUTE	DISTANCE	TIME

PACE	HEART RATE	WEATHER	SHOES

COMMENTS

ADDITIONAL RUN OR CROSS TRAINING			
TIME OF DAY	ROUTE	DISTANCE	TIME
PACE	HEART RATE	WEATHER	SHOES

COMMENTS

DAY 5

TIME OF DAY	ROUTE	DISTANCE	TIME
PACE	HEART RATE	WEATHER	SHOES

COMMENTS

ADDITIONAL RUN OR CROSS TRAINING			
TIME OF DAY	ROUTE	DISTANCE	TIME
PACE	HEART RATE	WEATHER	SHOES

COMMENTS

DAY 6

TIME OF DAY	ROUTE	DISTANCE	TIME
PACE	HEART RATE	WEATHER	SHOES

COMMENTS

ADDITIONAL RUN OR CROSS TRAINING			
TIME OF DAY	ROUTE	DISTANCE	TIME
PACE	HEART RATE	WEATHER	SHOES

COMMENTS

DAY 7	TIME OF DAY	ROUTE	DISTANCE	TIME
	PACE	HEART RATE	WEATHER	SHOES
	COMMENTS			

ADDITIONAL RUN OR CROSS TRAINING			
TIME OF DAY	ROUTE	DISTANCE	TIME
PACE	HEART RATE	WEATHER	SHOES
COMMENTS			

SUMMARY OF WEEK

RUNNING

TOTAL TIME

TOTAL DISTANCE

CROSS TRAINING

TOTAL TIME

TOTAL DISTANCE

STRENGTH & CONDITIONING

TOTAL TIME

REVIEW OF THE WEEK

HOW I FEEL PHYSICALLY

HOW I FEEL MENTALLY

HIGHLIGHTS OF THE WEEK

WEEK 13

DAY 1

TIME OF DAY	ROUTE	DISTANCE	TIME

PACE	HEART RATE	WEATHER	SHOES

COMMENTS

ADDITIONAL RUN OR CROSS TRAINING			
TIME OF DAY	ROUTE	DISTANCE	TIME
PACE	HEART RATE	WEATHER	SHOES

COMMENTS

DAY 2

TIME OF DAY	ROUTE	DISTANCE	TIME

PACE	HEART RATE	WEATHER	SHOES

COMMENTS

ADDITIONAL RUN OR CROSS TRAINING			
TIME OF DAY	ROUTE	DISTANCE	TIME
PACE	HEART RATE	WEATHER	SHOES

COMMENTS

DAY 3

TIME OF DAY	ROUTE	DISTANCE	TIME

PACE	HEART RATE	WEATHER	SHOES

COMMENTS

ADDITIONAL RUN OR CROSS TRAINING			
TIME OF DAY	ROUTE	DISTANCE	TIME
PACE	HEART RATE	WEATHER	SHOES

COMMENTS

DAY 4

TIME OF DAY	ROUTE	DISTANCE	TIME

PACE	HEART RATE	WEATHER	SHOES

COMMENTS

ADDITIONAL RUN OR CROSS TRAINING			
TIME OF DAY	ROUTE	DISTANCE	TIME
PACE	HEART RATE	WEATHER	SHOES

COMMENTS

DAY 5

TIME OF DAY	ROUTE	DISTANCE	TIME

PACE	HEART RATE	WEATHER	SHOES

COMMENTS

ADDITIONAL RUN OR CROSS TRAINING			
TIME OF DAY	ROUTE	DISTANCE	TIME
PACE	HEART RATE	WEATHER	SHOES

COMMENTS

DAY 6

TIME OF DAY	ROUTE	DISTANCE	TIME

PACE	HEART RATE	WEATHER	SHOES

COMMENTS

ADDITIONAL RUN OR CROSS TRAINING			
TIME OF DAY	ROUTE	DISTANCE	TIME
PACE	HEART RATE	WEATHER	SHOES

COMMENTS

DAY 7	TIME OF DAY	ROUTE	DISTANCE	TIME
	PACE	HEART RATE	WEATHER	SHOES

COMMENTS

ADDITIONAL RUN OR CROSS TRAINING			
TIME OF DAY	ROUTE	DISTANCE	TIME
PACE	HEART RATE	WEATHER	SHOES

COMMENTS

SUMMARY OF WEEK

RUNNING

TOTAL TIME	TOTAL DISTANCE

CROSS TRAINING

TOTAL TIME	TOTAL DISTANCE

STRENGTH & CONDITIONING

TOTAL TIME

REVIEW OF THE WEEK

HOW I FEEL PHYSICALLY

HOW I FEEL MENTALLY

HIGHLIGHTS OF THE WEEK

WEEK 14

DAY 1

TIME OF DAY	ROUTE	DISTANCE	TIME

PACE	HEART RATE	WEATHER	SHOES

COMMENTS

ADDITIONAL RUN OR CROSS TRAINING			
TIME OF DAY	ROUTE	DISTANCE	TIME
PACE	HEART RATE	WEATHER	SHOES

COMMENTS

DAY 2

TIME OF DAY	ROUTE	DISTANCE	TIME

PACE	HEART RATE	WEATHER	SHOES

COMMENTS

ADDITIONAL RUN OR CROSS TRAINING			
TIME OF DAY	ROUTE	DISTANCE	TIME
PACE	HEART RATE	WEATHER	SHOES

COMMENTS

DAY 3

TIME OF DAY	ROUTE	DISTANCE	TIME

PACE	HEART RATE	WEATHER	SHOES

COMMENTS

ADDITIONAL RUN OR CROSS TRAINING			
TIME OF DAY	ROUTE	DISTANCE	TIME
PACE	HEART RATE	WEATHER	SHOES

COMMENTS

DAY 4

TIME OF DAY	ROUTE	DISTANCE	TIME
PACE	HEART RATE	WEATHER	SHOES

COMMENTS

ADDITIONAL RUN OR CROSS TRAINING			
TIME OF DAY	ROUTE	DISTANCE	TIME
PACE	HEART RATE	WEATHER	SHOES

COMMENTS

DAY 5

TIME OF DAY	ROUTE	DISTANCE	TIME
PACE	HEART RATE	WEATHER	SHOES

COMMENTS

ADDITIONAL RUN OR CROSS TRAINING			
TIME OF DAY	ROUTE	DISTANCE	TIME
PACE	HEART RATE	WEATHER	SHOES

COMMENTS

DAY 6

TIME OF DAY	ROUTE	DISTANCE	TIME
PACE	HEART RATE	WEATHER	SHOES

COMMENTS

ADDITIONAL RUN OR CROSS TRAINING			
TIME OF DAY	ROUTE	DISTANCE	TIME
PACE	HEART RATE	WEATHER	SHOES

COMMENTS

	TIME OF DAY	ROUTE	DISTANCE	TIME
DAY 7				
	PACE	HEART RATE	WEATHER	SHOES
	COMMENTS			
	ADDITIONAL RUN OR CROSS TRAINING			
	TIME OF DAY	ROUTE	DISTANCE	TIME
	PACE	HEART RATE	WEATHER	SHOES
	COMMENTS			

SUMMARY OF WEEK

RUNNING

TOTAL TIME

TOTAL DISTANCE

CROSS TRAINING

TOTAL TIME

TOTAL DISTANCE

STRENGTH & CONDITIONING

TOTAL TIME

REVIEW OF THE WEEK

HOW I FEEL PHYSICALLY

HOW I FEEL MENTALLY

HIGHLIGHTS OF THE WEEK

WEEK 15

DAY 1

TIME OF DAY	ROUTE	DISTANCE	TIME

PACE	HEART RATE	WEATHER	SHOES

COMMENTS

ADDITIONAL RUN OR CROSS TRAINING			
TIME OF DAY	ROUTE	DISTANCE	TIME
PACE	HEART RATE	WEATHER	SHOES

COMMENTS

DAY 2

TIME OF DAY	ROUTE	DISTANCE	TIME
PACE	HEART RATE	WEATHER	SHOES

COMMENTS

ADDITIONAL RUN OR CROSS TRAINING			
TIME OF DAY	ROUTE	DISTANCE	TIME
PACE	HEART RATE	WEATHER	SHOES

COMMENTS

DAY 3

TIME OF DAY	ROUTE	DISTANCE	TIME

PACE	HEART RATE	WEATHER	SHOES

COMMENTS

ADDITIONAL RUN OR CROSS TRAINING			
TIME OF DAY	ROUTE	DISTANCE	TIME
PACE	HEART RATE	WEATHER	SHOES

COMMENTS

DAY 4

TIME OF DAY	ROUTE	DISTANCE	TIME

PACE	HEART RATE	WEATHER	SHOES

COMMENTS

ADDITIONAL RUN OR CROSS TRAINING			
TIME OF DAY	ROUTE	DISTANCE	TIME
PACE	HEART RATE	WEATHER	SHOES

COMMENTS

DAY 5

TIME OF DAY	ROUTE	DISTANCE	TIME

PACE	HEART RATE	WEATHER	SHOES

COMMENTS

ADDITIONAL RUN OR CROSS TRAINING			
TIME OF DAY	ROUTE	DISTANCE	TIME
PACE	HEART RATE	WEATHER	SHOES

COMMENTS

DAY 6

TIME OF DAY	ROUTE	DISTANCE	TIME

PACE	HEART RATE	WEATHER	SHOES

COMMENTS

ADDITIONAL RUN OR CROSS TRAINING			
TIME OF DAY	ROUTE	DISTANCE	TIME
PACE	HEART RATE	WEATHER	SHOES

COMMENTS

DAY 7	TIME OF DAY	ROUTE	DISTANCE	TIME
	PACE	HEART RATE	WEATHER	SHOES
	COMMENTS			

ADDITIONAL RUN OR CROSS TRAINING			
TIME OF DAY	ROUTE	DISTANCE	TIME
PACE	HEART RATE	WEATHER	SHOES
COMMENTS			

SUMMARY OF WEEK

RUNNING

TOTAL TIME

TOTAL DISTANCE

CROSS TRAINING

TOTAL TIME

TOTAL DISTANCE

STRENGTH & CONDITIONING

TOTAL TIME

REVIEW OF THE WEEK

HOW I FEEL PHYSICALLY

HOW I FEEL MENTALLY

HIGHLIGHTS OF THE WEEK

WEEK 16

DAY 1

TIME OF DAY	ROUTE	DISTANCE	TIME

PACE	HEART RATE	WEATHER	SHOES

COMMENTS

ADDITIONAL RUN OR CROSS TRAINING			
TIME OF DAY	ROUTE	DISTANCE	TIME
PACE	HEART RATE	WEATHER	SHOES

COMMENTS

DAY 2

TIME OF DAY	ROUTE	DISTANCE	TIME

PACE	HEART RATE	WEATHER	SHOES

COMMENTS

ADDITIONAL RUN OR CROSS TRAINING			
TIME OF DAY	ROUTE	DISTANCE	TIME
PACE	HEART RATE	WEATHER	SHOES

COMMENTS

DAY 3

TIME OF DAY	ROUTE	DISTANCE	TIME

PACE	HEART RATE	WEATHER	SHOES

COMMENTS

ADDITIONAL RUN OR CROSS TRAINING			
TIME OF DAY	ROUTE	DISTANCE	TIME
PACE	HEART RATE	WEATHER	SHOES

COMMENTS

DAY 4

TIME OF DAY	ROUTE	DISTANCE	TIME

PACE	HEART RATE	WEATHER	SHOES

COMMENTS

ADDITIONAL RUN OR CROSS TRAINING			
TIME OF DAY	ROUTE	DISTANCE	TIME
PACE	HEART RATE	WEATHER	SHOES

COMMENTS

DAY 5

TIME OF DAY	ROUTE	DISTANCE	TIME

PACE	HEART RATE	WEATHER	SHOES

COMMENTS

ADDITIONAL RUN OR CROSS TRAINING			
TIME OF DAY	ROUTE	DISTANCE	TIME
PACE	HEART RATE	WEATHER	SHOES

COMMENTS

DAY 6

TIME OF DAY	ROUTE	DISTANCE	TIME

PACE	HEART RATE	WEATHER	SHOES

COMMENTS

ADDITIONAL RUN OR CROSS TRAINING			
TIME OF DAY	ROUTE	DISTANCE	TIME
PACE	HEART RATE	WEATHER	SHOES

COMMENTS

DAY 7	TIME OF DAY	ROUTE	DISTANCE	TIME
	PACE	HEART RATE	WEATHER	SHOES

COMMENTS

ADDITIONAL RUN OR CROSS TRAINING			
TIME OF DAY	ROUTE	DISTANCE	TIME
PACE	HEART RATE	WEATHER	SHOES

COMMENTS

SUMMARY OF WEEK

RUNNING

TOTAL TIME   TOTAL DISTANCE

CROSS TRAINING

TOTAL TIME   TOTAL DISTANCE

STRENGTH & CONDITIONING

TOTAL TIME

REVIEW OF THE WEEK

HOW I FEEL PHYSICALLY

HOW I FEEL MENTALLY

HIGHLIGHTS OF THE WEEK

WEEK 17

DAY 1

TIME OF DAY	ROUTE	DISTANCE	TIME

PACE	HEART RATE	WEATHER	SHOES

COMMENTS

ADDITIONAL RUN OR CROSS TRAINING			
TIME OF DAY	ROUTE	DISTANCE	TIME
PACE	HEART RATE	WEATHER	SHOES

COMMENTS

DAY 2

TIME OF DAY	ROUTE	DISTANCE	TIME

PACE	HEART RATE	WEATHER	SHOES

COMMENTS

ADDITIONAL RUN OR CROSS TRAINING			
TIME OF DAY	ROUTE	DISTANCE	TIME
PACE	HEART RATE	WEATHER	SHOES

COMMENTS

DAY 3

TIME OF DAY	ROUTE	DISTANCE	TIME

PACE	HEART RATE	WEATHER	SHOES

COMMENTS

ADDITIONAL RUN OR CROSS TRAINING			
TIME OF DAY	ROUTE	DISTANCE	TIME
PACE	HEART RATE	WEATHER	SHOES

COMMENTS

DAY 4

TIME OF DAY	ROUTE	DISTANCE	TIME

PACE	HEART RATE	WEATHER	SHOES

COMMENTS

ADDITIONAL RUN OR CROSS TRAINING			
TIME OF DAY	ROUTE	DISTANCE	TIME
PACE	HEART RATE	WEATHER	SHOES

COMMENTS

DAY 5

TIME OF DAY	ROUTE	DISTANCE	TIME

PACE	HEART RATE	WEATHER	SHOES

COMMENTS

ADDITIONAL RUN OR CROSS TRAINING			
TIME OF DAY	ROUTE	DISTANCE	TIME
PACE	HEART RATE	WEATHER	SHOES

COMMENTS

DAY 6

TIME OF DAY	ROUTE	DISTANCE	TIME

PACE	HEART RATE	WEATHER	SHOES

COMMENTS

ADDITIONAL RUN OR CROSS TRAINING			
TIME OF DAY	ROUTE	DISTANCE	TIME
PACE	HEART RATE	WEATHER	SHOES

COMMENTS

DAY 7	TIME OF DAY	ROUTE	DISTANCE	TIME
	PACE	HEART RATE	WEATHER	SHOES
	COMMENTS			

ADDITIONAL RUN OR CROSS TRAINING			
TIME OF DAY	ROUTE	DISTANCE	TIME
PACE	HEART RATE	WEATHER	SHOES
COMMENTS			

SUMMARY OF WEEK

RUNNING

TOTAL TIME

TOTAL DISTANCE

CROSS TRAINING

TOTAL TIME

TOTAL DISTANCE

STRENGTH & CONDITIONING

TOTAL TIME

REVIEW OF THE WEEK

HOW I FEEL PHYSICALLY

HOW I FEEL MENTALLY

HIGHLIGHTS OF THE WEEK

WEEK 18

DAY 1

TIME OF DAY	ROUTE	DISTANCE	TIME
PACE	HEART RATE	WEATHER	SHOES

COMMENTS

ADDITIONAL RUN OR CROSS TRAINING			
TIME OF DAY	ROUTE	DISTANCE	TIME
PACE	HEART RATE	WEATHER	SHOES

COMMENTS

DAY 2

TIME OF DAY	ROUTE	DISTANCE	TIME
PACE	HEART RATE	WEATHER	SHOES

COMMENTS

ADDITIONAL RUN OR CROSS TRAINING			
TIME OF DAY	ROUTE	DISTANCE	TIME
PACE	HEART RATE	WEATHER	SHOES

COMMENTS

DAY 3

TIME OF DAY	ROUTE	DISTANCE	TIME

PACE	HEART RATE	WEATHER	SHOES

COMMENTS

ADDITIONAL RUN OR CROSS TRAINING

TIME OF DAY	ROUTE	DISTANCE	TIME

PACE	HEART RATE	WEATHER	SHOES

COMMENTS

DAY 4

TIME OF DAY	ROUTE	DISTANCE	TIME

PACE	HEART RATE	WEATHER	SHOES

COMMENTS

ADDITIONAL RUN OR CROSS TRAINING

TIME OF DAY	ROUTE	DISTANCE	TIME

PACE	HEART RATE	WEATHER	SHOES

COMMENTS

DAY 5

TIME OF DAY	ROUTE	DISTANCE	TIME
PACE	HEART RATE	WEATHER	SHOES

COMMENTS

ADDITIONAL RUN OR CROSS TRAINING			
TIME OF DAY	ROUTE	DISTANCE	TIME
PACE	HEART RATE	WEATHER	SHOES

COMMENTS

DAY 6

TIME OF DAY	ROUTE	DISTANCE	TIME
PACE	HEART RATE	WEATHER	SHOES

COMMENTS

ADDITIONAL RUN OR CROSS TRAINING			
TIME OF DAY	ROUTE	DISTANCE	TIME
PACE	HEART RATE	WEATHER	SHOES

COMMENTS

DAY 7	TIME OF DAY	ROUTE	DISTANCE	TIME
	PACE	HEART RATE	WEATHER	SHOES
	COMMENTS			

ADDITIONAL RUN OR CROSS TRAINING

TIME OF DAY	ROUTE	DISTANCE	TIME
PACE	HEART RATE	WEATHER	SHOES
COMMENTS			

SUMMARY OF WEEK

RUNNING

TOTAL TIME	TOTAL DISTANCE

CROSS TRAINING

TOTAL TIME	TOTAL DISTANCE

STRENGTH & CONDITIONING

TOTAL TIME

REVIEW OF THE WEEK

HOW I FEEL PHYSICALLY

HOW I FEEL MENTALLY

HIGHLIGHTS OF THE WEEK

WEEK 19

DAY 1

TIME OF DAY	ROUTE	DISTANCE	TIME
PACE	HEART RATE	WEATHER	SHOES

COMMENTS

ADDITIONAL RUN OR CROSS TRAINING			
TIME OF DAY	ROUTE	DISTANCE	TIME
PACE	HEART RATE	WEATHER	SHOES

COMMENTS

DAY 2

TIME OF DAY	ROUTE	DISTANCE	TIME
PACE	HEART RATE	WEATHER	SHOES

COMMENTS

ADDITIONAL RUN OR CROSS TRAINING			
TIME OF DAY	ROUTE	DISTANCE	TIME
PACE	HEART RATE	WEATHER	SHOES

COMMENTS

DAY 3

TIME OF DAY	ROUTE	DISTANCE	TIME

PACE	HEART RATE	WEATHER	SHOES

COMMENTS

ADDITIONAL RUN OR CROSS TRAINING			
TIME OF DAY	ROUTE	DISTANCE	TIME
PACE	HEART RATE	WEATHER	SHOES

COMMENTS

DAY 4

TIME OF DAY	ROUTE	DISTANCE	TIME

PACE	HEART RATE	WEATHER	SHOES

COMMENTS

ADDITIONAL RUN OR CROSS TRAINING			
TIME OF DAY	ROUTE	DISTANCE	TIME
PACE	HEART RATE	WEATHER	SHOES

COMMENTS

DAY 5

TIME OF DAY	ROUTE	DISTANCE	TIME
PACE	HEART RATE	WEATHER	SHOES

COMMENTS

ADDITIONAL RUN OR CROSS TRAINING			
TIME OF DAY	ROUTE	DISTANCE	TIME
PACE	HEART RATE	WEATHER	SHOES

COMMENTS

DAY 6

TIME OF DAY	ROUTE	DISTANCE	TIME
PACE	HEART RATE	WEATHER	SHOES

COMMENTS

ADDITIONAL RUN OR CROSS TRAINING			
TIME OF DAY	ROUTE	DISTANCE	TIME
PACE	HEART RATE	WEATHER	SHOES

COMMENTS

DAY 7	TIME OF DAY	ROUTE	DISTANCE	TIME
	PACE	HEART RATE	WEATHER	SHOES

COMMENTS

ADDITIONAL RUN OR CROSS TRAINING			
TIME OF DAY	ROUTE	DISTANCE	TIME
PACE	HEART RATE	WEATHER	SHOES

COMMENTS

SUMMARY OF WEEK

RUNNING

TOTAL TIME

TOTAL DISTANCE

CROSS TRAINING

TOTAL TIME

TOTAL DISTANCE

STRENGTH & CONDITIONING

TOTAL TIME

REVIEW OF THE WEEK

HOW I FEEL PHYSICALLY

HOW I FEEL MENTALLY

HIGHLIGHTS OF THE WEEK

WEEK 20

DAY 1

TIME OF DAY	ROUTE	DISTANCE	TIME
PACE	HEART RATE	WEATHER	SHOES

COMMENTS

ADDITIONAL RUN OR CROSS TRAINING			
TIME OF DAY	ROUTE	DISTANCE	TIME
PACE	HEART RATE	WEATHER	SHOES

COMMENTS

DAY 2

TIME OF DAY	ROUTE	DISTANCE	TIME
PACE	HEART RATE	WEATHER	SHOES

COMMENTS

ADDITIONAL RUN OR CROSS TRAINING			
TIME OF DAY	ROUTE	DISTANCE	TIME
PACE	HEART RATE	WEATHER	SHOES

COMMENTS

DAY 3

TIME OF DAY	ROUTE	DISTANCE	TIME
PACE	HEART RATE	WEATHER	SHOES

COMMENTS

ADDITIONAL RUN OR CROSS TRAINING			
TIME OF DAY	ROUTE	DISTANCE	TIME
PACE	HEART RATE	WEATHER	SHOES

COMMENTS

DAY 4

TIME OF DAY	ROUTE	DISTANCE	TIME
PACE	HEART RATE	WEATHER	SHOES

COMMENTS

ADDITIONAL RUN OR CROSS TRAINING			
TIME OF DAY	ROUTE	DISTANCE	TIME
PACE	HEART RATE	WEATHER	SHOES

COMMENTS

DAY 5

TIME OF DAY	ROUTE	DISTANCE	TIME

PACE	HEART RATE	WEATHER	SHOES

COMMENTS

ADDITIONAL RUN OR CROSS TRAINING			
TIME OF DAY	ROUTE	DISTANCE	TIME
PACE	HEART RATE	WEATHER	SHOES

COMMENTS

DAY 6

TIME OF DAY	ROUTE	DISTANCE	TIME

PACE	HEART RATE	WEATHER	SHOES

COMMENTS

ADDITIONAL RUN OR CROSS TRAINING			
TIME OF DAY	ROUTE	DISTANCE	TIME
PACE	HEART RATE	WEATHER	SHOES

COMMENTS

DAY 7	TIME OF DAY	ROUTE	DISTANCE	TIME
	PACE	HEART RATE	WEATHER	SHOES

COMMENTS

ADDITIONAL RUN OR CROSS TRAINING			
TIME OF DAY	ROUTE	DISTANCE	TIME
PACE	HEART RATE	WEATHER	SHOES

COMMENTS

SUMMARY OF WEEK

RUNNING

TOTAL TIME	TOTAL DISTANCE

CROSS TRAINING

TOTAL TIME	TOTAL DISTANCE

STRENGTH & CONDITIONING

TOTAL TIME

REVIEW OF THE WEEK

HOW I FEEL PHYSICALLY

HOW I FEEL MENTALLY

HIGHLIGHTS OF THE WEEK

WEEK 21

DAY 1

TIME OF DAY	ROUTE	DISTANCE	TIME

PACE	HEART RATE	WEATHER	SHOES

COMMENTS

ADDITIONAL RUN OR CROSS TRAINING			
TIME OF DAY	ROUTE	DISTANCE	TIME
PACE	HEART RATE	WEATHER	SHOES

COMMENTS

DAY 2

TIME OF DAY	ROUTE	DISTANCE	TIME
PACE	HEART RATE	WEATHER	SHOES

COMMENTS

ADDITIONAL RUN OR CROSS TRAINING			
TIME OF DAY	ROUTE	DISTANCE	TIME
PACE	HEART RATE	WEATHER	SHOES

COMMENTS

DAY 3

TIME OF DAY	ROUTE	DISTANCE	TIME

PACE	HEART RATE	WEATHER	SHOES

COMMENTS

ADDITIONAL RUN OR CROSS TRAINING			
TIME OF DAY	ROUTE	DISTANCE	TIME
PACE	HEART RATE	WEATHER	SHOES

COMMENTS

DAY 4

TIME OF DAY	ROUTE	DISTANCE	TIME

PACE	HEART RATE	WEATHER	SHOES

COMMENTS

ADDITIONAL RUN OR CROSS TRAINING			
TIME OF DAY	ROUTE	DISTANCE	TIME
PACE	HEART RATE	WEATHER	SHOES

COMMENTS

DAY 5

TIME OF DAY	ROUTE	DISTANCE	TIME

PACE	HEART RATE	WEATHER	SHOES

COMMENTS

ADDITIONAL RUN OR CROSS TRAINING			
TIME OF DAY	ROUTE	DISTANCE	TIME
PACE	HEART RATE	WEATHER	SHOES

COMMENTS

DAY 6

TIME OF DAY	ROUTE	DISTANCE	TIME

PACE	HEART RATE	WEATHER	SHOES

COMMENTS

ADDITIONAL RUN OR CROSS TRAINING			
TIME OF DAY	ROUTE	DISTANCE	TIME
PACE	HEART RATE	WEATHER	SHOES

COMMENTS

DAY 7	TIME OF DAY	ROUTE	DISTANCE	TIME
	PACE	HEART RATE	WEATHER	SHOES

COMMENTS

ADDITIONAL RUN OR CROSS TRAINING			
TIME OF DAY	ROUTE	DISTANCE	TIME
PACE	HEART RATE	WEATHER	SHOES

COMMENTS

SUMMARY OF WEEK

RUNNING

TOTAL TIME	TOTAL DISTANCE

CROSS TRAINING

TOTAL TIME	TOTAL DISTANCE

STRENGTH & CONDITIONING

TOTAL TIME

REVIEW OF THE WEEK

HOW I FEEL PHYSICALLY

HOW I FEEL MENTALLY

HIGHLIGHTS OF THE WEEK

WEEK 22

DAY 1

TIME OF DAY	ROUTE	DISTANCE	TIME

PACE	HEART RATE	WEATHER	SHOES

COMMENTS

ADDITIONAL RUN OR CROSS TRAINING			
TIME OF DAY	ROUTE	DISTANCE	TIME
PACE	HEART RATE	WEATHER	SHOES

COMMENTS

DAY 2

TIME OF DAY	ROUTE	DISTANCE	TIME

PACE	HEART RATE	WEATHER	SHOES

COMMENTS

ADDITIONAL RUN OR CROSS TRAINING			
TIME OF DAY	ROUTE	DISTANCE	TIME
PACE	HEART RATE	WEATHER	SHOES

COMMENTS

DAY 3

TIME OF DAY	ROUTE	DISTANCE	TIME

PACE	HEART RATE	WEATHER	SHOES

COMMENTS

ADDITIONAL RUN OR CROSS TRAINING			
TIME OF DAY	ROUTE	DISTANCE	TIME
PACE	HEART RATE	WEATHER	SHOES

COMMENTS

DAY 4

TIME OF DAY	ROUTE	DISTANCE	TIME

PACE	HEART RATE	WEATHER	SHOES

COMMENTS

ADDITIONAL RUN OR CROSS TRAINING			
TIME OF DAY	ROUTE	DISTANCE	TIME
PACE	HEART RATE	WEATHER	SHOES

COMMENTS

DAY 5

TIME OF DAY	ROUTE	DISTANCE	TIME

PACE	HEART RATE	WEATHER	SHOES

COMMENTS

ADDITIONAL RUN OR CROSS TRAINING			
TIME OF DAY	ROUTE	DISTANCE	TIME
PACE	HEART RATE	WEATHER	SHOES

COMMENTS

DAY 6

TIME OF DAY	ROUTE	DISTANCE	TIME
PACE	HEART RATE	WEATHER	SHOES

COMMENTS

ADDITIONAL RUN OR CROSS TRAINING			
TIME OF DAY	ROUTE	DISTANCE	TIME
PACE	HEART RATE	WEATHER	SHOES

COMMENTS

DAY 7	TIME OF DAY	ROUTE	DISTANCE	TIME
	PACE	HEART RATE	WEATHER	SHOES
	COMMENTS			
	ADDITIONAL RUN OR CROSS TRAINING			
	TIME OF DAY	ROUTE	DISTANCE	TIME
	PACE	HEART RATE	WEATHER	SHOES
	COMMENTS			

SUMMARY OF WEEK

RUNNING

TOTAL TIME	TOTAL DISTANCE

CROSS TRAINING

TOTAL TIME	TOTAL DISTANCE

STRENGTH & CONDITIONING

TOTAL TIME

REVIEW OF THE WEEK

HOW I FEEL PHYSICALLY

HOW I FEEL MENTALLY

HIGHLIGHTS OF THE WEEK

WEEK 23

DAY 1

TIME OF DAY	ROUTE	DISTANCE	TIME

PACE	HEART RATE	WEATHER	SHOES

COMMENTS

ADDITIONAL RUN OR CROSS TRAINING			
TIME OF DAY	ROUTE	DISTANCE	TIME
PACE	HEART RATE	WEATHER	SHOES

COMMENTS

DAY 2

TIME OF DAY	ROUTE	DISTANCE	TIME

PACE	HEART RATE	WEATHER	SHOES

COMMENTS

ADDITIONAL RUN OR CROSS TRAINING			
TIME OF DAY	ROUTE	DISTANCE	TIME
PACE	HEART RATE	WEATHER	SHOES

COMMENTS

DAY 3

TIME OF DAY	ROUTE	DISTANCE	TIME

PACE	HEART RATE	WEATHER	SHOES

COMMENTS

ADDITIONAL RUN OR CROSS TRAINING			
TIME OF DAY	ROUTE	DISTANCE	TIME
PACE	HEART RATE	WEATHER	SHOES

COMMENTS

DAY 4

TIME OF DAY	ROUTE	DISTANCE	TIME
PACE	HEART RATE	WEATHER	SHOES

COMMENTS

ADDITIONAL RUN OR CROSS TRAINING			
TIME OF DAY	ROUTE	DISTANCE	TIME
PACE	HEART RATE	WEATHER	SHOES

COMMENTS

DAY 5

TIME OF DAY	ROUTE	DISTANCE	TIME

PACE	HEART RATE	WEATHER	SHOES

COMMENTS

ADDITIONAL RUN OR CROSS TRAINING			
TIME OF DAY	ROUTE	DISTANCE	TIME
PACE	HEART RATE	WEATHER	SHOES

COMMENTS

DAY 6

TIME OF DAY	ROUTE	DISTANCE	TIME

PACE	HEART RATE	WEATHER	SHOES

COMMENTS

ADDITIONAL RUN OR CROSS TRAINING			
TIME OF DAY	ROUTE	DISTANCE	TIME
PACE	HEART RATE	WEATHER	SHOES

COMMENTS

DAY 7	TIME OF DAY	ROUTE	DISTANCE	TIME
	PACE	HEART RATE	WEATHER	SHOES
	COMMENTS			

ADDITIONAL RUN OR CROSS TRAINING			
TIME OF DAY	ROUTE	DISTANCE	TIME
PACE	HEART RATE	WEATHER	SHOES
COMMENTS			

SUMMARY OF WEEK

RUNNING

TOTAL TIME	TOTAL DISTANCE

CROSS TRAINING

TOTAL TIME	TOTAL DISTANCE

STRENGTH & CONDITIONING

TOTAL TIME

REVIEW OF THE WEEK

HOW I FEEL PHYSICALLY

HOW I FEEL MENTALLY

HIGHLIGHTS OF THE WEEK

MY RACE DAY PLAN

RACE DAY KIT

RACE DAY NUTRITION

RACE DAY PACING PLAN

WEEK 24

DAY 1

TIME OF DAY	ROUTE	DISTANCE	TIME

PACE	HEART RATE	WEATHER	SHOES

COMMENTS

ADDITIONAL RUN OR CROSS TRAINING			
TIME OF DAY	ROUTE	DISTANCE	TIME
PACE	HEART RATE	WEATHER	SHOES

COMMENTS

DAY 2

TIME OF DAY	ROUTE	DISTANCE	TIME
PACE	HEART RATE	WEATHER	SHOES

COMMENTS

ADDITIONAL RUN OR CROSS TRAINING			
TIME OF DAY	ROUTE	DISTANCE	TIME
PACE	HEART RATE	WEATHER	SHOES

COMMENTS

DAY 3

TIME OF DAY	ROUTE	DISTANCE	TIME

PACE	HEART RATE	WEATHER	SHOES

COMMENTS

ADDITIONAL RUN OR CROSS TRAINING			
TIME OF DAY	ROUTE	DISTANCE	TIME
PACE	HEART RATE	WEATHER	SHOES

COMMENTS

DAY 4

TIME OF DAY	ROUTE	DISTANCE	TIME

PACE	HEART RATE	WEATHER	SHOES

COMMENTS

ADDITIONAL RUN OR CROSS TRAINING			
TIME OF DAY	ROUTE	DISTANCE	TIME
PACE	HEART RATE	WEATHER	SHOES

COMMENTS

DAY 5

TIME OF DAY	ROUTE	DISTANCE	TIME

PACE	HEART RATE	WEATHER	SHOES

COMMENTS

ADDITIONAL RUN OR CROSS TRAINING			
TIME OF DAY	ROUTE	DISTANCE	TIME
PACE	HEART RATE	WEATHER	SHOES
COMMENTS			

DAY 6

TIME OF DAY	ROUTE	DISTANCE	TIME

PACE	HEART RATE	WEATHER	SHOES

COMMENTS

ADDITIONAL RUN OR CROSS TRAINING			
TIME OF DAY	ROUTE	DISTANCE	TIME
PACE	HEART RATE	WEATHER	SHOES
COMMENTS			

DAY 7	TIME OF DAY	ROUTE	DISTANCE	TIME
	PACE	HEART RATE	WEATHER	SHOES
	COMMENTS			

ADDITIONAL RUN OR CROSS TRAINING			
TIME OF DAY	ROUTE	DISTANCE	TIME
PACE	HEART RATE	WEATHER	SHOES
COMMENTS			

SUMMARY OF WEEK

RUNNING

TOTAL TIME	TOTAL DISTANCE

CROSS TRAINING

TOTAL TIME	TOTAL DISTANCE

STRENGTH & CONDITIONING

TOTAL TIME

REVIEW OF THE WEEK

HOW I FEEL PHYSICALLY

HOW I FEEL MENTALLY

HIGHLIGHTS OF THE WEEK

RACE RESULT

FINISHING TIME

FINISHING POSITION

AGE GROUP FINISHING POSITION

RACE EVALUATION

WHAT WENT WELL

WHAT DID NOT GO WELL

WHAT I WILL CHANGE NEXT TIME

TRAINING BLOCK EVALUATION

WHAT WENT WELL

WHAT DID NOT GO WELL

WHAT I WILL CHANGE NEXT TIME

MY RACE PHOTO

MY RACE NUMBER

Printed in Great Britain
by Amazon